The Artful Cat

BEAU
Esther Walton
. . . .

THE Artful Cat

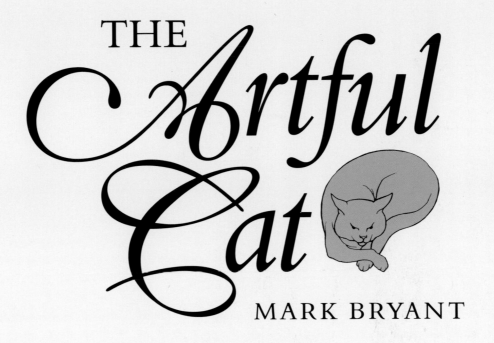

MARK BRYANT

COURAGE
BOOKS
AN IMPRINT OF
RUNNING PRESS
PHILADELPHIA, PENNSYLVANIA

A QUARTO BOOK

Copyright 1991
Quarto Publishing plc

9 8 7 6 5 4 3 2

Digit on the right indicates the number of this printing.

Library of Congress Cataloging-in-Publication Number 91-71638

ISBN 1-56138-061-X

This book was designed and produced by
Quarto Publishing plc
6, Blundell Street
London N7 9BH

Art Director *Moira Clinch*
Art Editor *Philip Gilderdale*
Designer *Fiona Russell*
Senior Editor *Hazel Harrison*
Picture Researcher *Jane Lambert*

Typeset in Great Britain by ABC Typesetters, Bournemouth
Manufactured in Singapore by Chroma Graphics (Overseas) Pte. Ltd.
Printed in Hong Kong by Leefung-Asco Printers Limited
First Published in the United States by Courage Books, an imprint of Running Press
Book Publishers
125 South Twenty-second Street
Philadelphia, Pennsylvania 19103

CONTENTS

INTRODUCTION

— *page 7* —

CHAPTER ONE

Catlings and Kittens

— *page 9* —

CHAPTER TWO

The Sphinx

— *page 31* —

CHAPTER THREE

Tiger! Tiger!

— *page 61* —

CHAPTER FOUR

A Clowder of Cats

— *page 91* —

CHAPTER FIVE

Requiescat

— *page 111* —

INTRODUCTION

*W*hether your cat resembles Thomas Hardy's "dumb friend" who waits "to meet the stroking hand" or is more like Kipling's independent cat, "walking by his wild lone," your fireside companion will unquestionably possess that remarkable combination of wisdom and style rarely present in any other animal – humans included.

This book is a celebration of the cat in words and pictures by those who have been lovers, students, victims, admirers, and not infrequently, slaves of the beguiling household sphinx in its many moods and incarnations.

Some of the world's finest creative talents have applied their pens, paintbrushes, and typewriters to capturing the essential artfulness of the cat. From savage tiger to playful kitten, and from serene Buddha to domestic dictator, all manner of cats is portrayed in this volume.

Mark Bryant

PORTRAIT OF THOMAS
Pippa Sterne
. . . .

CHAPTER ONE

Catlings and Kittens

A kitten is in the animal world what a rosebud
is in a garden. *Robert Southey*

THREE WHITE ANGORA KITTENS
Arthur Heyer
. . . .

little lion, small and dainty sweet...
With sea-grey eyes and softly stepping feet...

GRAHAM R. TOMSON (1863-1911)
From 'Arsinoë's cats'

PUSSY IN THE WORKBASKET
(Artist unknown)
. . . .

COULD MY PUSSY SPEAK, SHE WOULD SAY
I WISH YOU A HAPPY CHRISTMAS-DAY.

The hapless Nymph with wonder saw:

A whisker first, and then a claw,

With many an ardent wish,

She stretch'd in vain to reach the prize.

What female heart can gold despise?

What cat's averse to fish?

THOMAS GRAY (1716–71)
From 'On the Death of a Favourite Cat, Drowned
in a Tub of Gold Fishes'

THE FISHING PARTY
Horatio Henry Couldrey

It's very nice to think of how
In every country lives a Cow
To furnish milk with all her might
For Kittens' comfort and delight.

OLIVER HERFORD (1863-1935)
'A Thought'

FELINES AT PLAY
B. B.

14

*D*o you see that kitten chasing so prettily her own tail? If you could look with her eyes, you might see her surrounded with hundreds of figures performing complex dramas, with tragic and comic issues, long conversations, many characters, many ups and downs of fate.

RALPH WALDO EMERSON (1803-82)
From *Experience*

MISS ANN WHITE'S KITTEN
George Stubbs

When I grow up I mean to be

A Lion large and fierce to see.

I'll mew so loud that Cook in fright

Will give me all the cream in sight.

And anyone who dares to say

'Poor Puss' to me will rue the day.

Then having swallowed him I'll creep

Into the Guest Bed Room to sleep.

OLIVER HERFORD (1863–1935)
'Anticipation'

WHO'S THE FAIREST OF THEM ALL?
Frank Paton

She is a sprightly cat, hardly past her youth... she darts out a paw, and begins plucking it and inquiring into the matter, as if it were a challenge to play, or something lively enough to be eaten. What a graceful action of that foot of hers, between delicacy and petulance! – combining something of a thrust out, a beat and a scratch.

LEIGH HUNT (1784-1859)
From 'The Cat by the Fire'

KITTEN AND BALL OF WOOL
Murata Kokoku

Our old cat has kittens three

And what do you think their names shall be?

Pepperpot, Sootikins, Scratch-away-there,

Was there ever a kitten with these to compare?

And we call their old mother – now, what do you think?

Tabitha Long-claws Tiddley-wink!

TOM HOOD (1835-74)
From 'Choosing Their Names'

THE FACE AT THE WINDOW
Fannie Moody

In a cat's eyes, all things belong to cats.

ENGLISH SAYING

KITTENS AT A BANQUET
Louis Eugene Lambert

*K*itten, you are very little,
And your kitten bones are brittle,
If you'd grow to Cats respected,
See your play be not neglected.

Smite the Sudden Spool, and spring
Upon the Swift Elusive String,
Thus you learn to catch the wary
Mister Mouse or Miss Canary.

OLIVER HERFORD (1863-1935)
From *The Kitten's Garden of Verses*

KITTEN
Emma Goss
. . . .

Four-Paws, the kitten from the farm,
Is come to live with Betsy Jane,
Leaving the stack-yard for the warm
Flower-compassed cottage in the lane,
To wash his idle face and play
Among chintz cushions all the day.

Under the shadow of her hair
He lies, who loves him, nor desists
To praise his whiskers and compare
The tabby bracelets on his wrists –
Omelette at lunch, and milk at tea
Suits Betsy Jane, and so fares he.

H PARRY EDEN
From 'Four-Paws'
. . . .

KITTEN ON CUSHIONS
Sally Holmes
. . . .

CHAPTER TWO

The Sphinx

And when the moon gets up and night comes,
he is the Cat that walks by himself, and all
places are alike to him. *Rudyard Kipling*

TABBY CAT
Artist Unknown
. . . .

Stately, kindly, lordly friend,

Condescend

Here to sit by me, and turn

Glorious eyes that smile and burn,

Golden eyes, love's lustrous meed,

On the golden page I read.

All your wondrous wealth of hair,

Dark and fair,

Silken-shaggy, soft and bright

As the clouds and beams of night,

Pays my reverent hand's caress

Back with friendlier gentleness.

ALGERNON SWINBURNE (1837-1909)
From 'To a Cat'

CAT
E. B. Watts
. . . .

E.B.Watts '80.

You see the beauty of the world
    Through eyes of unalloyed content,
And in my study chair upcurled,
Move me to pensive wonderment.

I wish I knew your trick of thought,
    The perfect balance of your ways;
They seem an inspiration, caught
From other laws in older days.

ANONYMOUS
in *The Spectator*

CAT ON A RUSH CHAIR
Sei Koyanagui
. . . .

My tribe are sure that creation's plan

Meant *us* for the genuine super-man:

When you prate of your Nietzsches and Bernard Shaws,

With a dainty smile we lick our paws:

For thousands of years we have known all that –

Saith Simon the Black, my cat.

SIR FREDERICK POLLOCK (1845-1937)
From 'Niger Sed Sapiens'

SLEEPY CAT
Eileen Mayo

. . . .

Sleepy Cat 29/60   Eileen Mayo

uddy is the oldest of the cats. Mostly she sits by the fireside and dreams her dreams. I imagine that she has come to agree with the philosopher that the eye and the ear and the other senses are full of deceit. More and more her mind dwells on the invisible.

SIR OLIVER LODGE (1851-1940)
Quoted in *Children of the Moon* by Moira Meighn

FELINE PHANTASY
Enid Marx

Feline Phantasy   14/50   Enid Marx

A poet's cat, sedate and grave,
As poet well could wish to have,
Was much addicted to inquire
For nooks, to which she might retire,
And where, secure as mouse in chink,
She might repose, or sit and think.
I know not where she caught the trick –
Nature perhaps herself had cast her
In such a mould philosophique,
Or else she learn'd it of her master.

WILLIAM COWPER (1731–1800)
From 'The Retired Cat'

MY BATHROOM CAT
Ditz
. . . .

Far down within the damp dark earth

The grimy miner goes

That I on chilly nights may have

A fire to warm my toes;

Brave sailors plow the wintry main

Through peril and mishap,

That I, on Oriental rugs

May take my morning nap.

Out in the distant meadow

Meekly graze the lowing kine,

That milk in endless saucerfuls,

All foaming, may be mine;

The fish that swim the ocean

And the birds that fill the air –

Did I not like to pick their bones,

Pray, think you they'd be there?

ANONYMOUS
From 'A Modest Cat's Soliloquy'

WINSTON WITH ANEMONES
Rosalind Stoddart

Cruel, but composed and bland,
Dumb, inscrutable and grand,
So Tiberius might have sat,
Had Tiberius been a cat.

MATTHEW ARNOLD (1822-88)
From 'Poor Matthias'

CAT ON A WINDOW SILL
Joan Freestone

. . . .

Thou art the Great Cat, the avenger of the Gods, and the judge of words, and the president of the sovereign chiefs and the governor of the holy Circle; thou art indeed...the Great Cat.

From '75 Praises of Ra' inscribed on the walls of the royal tombs at Thebes

LUCY
Martin Leman
. . . .

On some grave business, soft and slow

Along the garden paths you go

With bold and burning eyes,

Or stand with twitching tail to mark

What starts and rustles in the dark

Among the peonies.

A. C. BENSON (1862-1925)
'The Cat'

GOLFING CAT
Hilary Jones
. . . .

It has a broad Face almost like a Lyon, short Ears, large Whiskers, shining Eyes, short smooth Hair, long Tail, rough Tongue, and armed on its Feet with Claws. . . . As to its Eyes, Authors say that they shine in the Night, and see better at the full, and more dimly at the change of the Moon. . . .

WILLIAM SALMON
From *The Dimunitive Lyon or Catus, the Cat*

ILLUSTRATION FROM THE HISTORIE OF
FOURE-FOOTED BEASTES
Edward Topsell

*L*ong contact with the human race has developed in it the art of diplomacy, and no Roman Cardinal of mediaeval days knew better how to ingratiate himself with his surroundings than a cat with a saucer of cream on its mental horizon.

'SAKI' (1870-1916)
From 'The Achievement of the Cat'

DEUX CHATS ENDORMIS
T. L. Foujita

The cat went here and there
And the moon spun round like a top,
And the nearest kin of the moon,
The creeping cat, looked up.
Black Minnaloushe stared at the moon,
For, wander and wail as he would,
The pure cold light in the sky
Troubled his animal blood.
Minnaloushe runs in the grass
Lifting his delicate feet.
Do you dance, Minnaloushe, do you dance?

WILLIAM BUTLER YEATS (1865-1939)
'The Cat and the Moon'

YOUTH
Will Barnet

If man could be crossed with the cat it would improve man, but it would deteriorate the cat.

MARK TWAIN (1835–1910)

PUSS IN BOOTS
Artist unknown
. . . .

PUSS
IN
BOOTS

*S*phinx of my quiet hearth

Thou deignst to dwell,

Friend of my toil, companion of my ease,

Thine is the lore of Ra and Rameses;

That men forget thou dost remember well,

Beholden still in blinking reveries,

With sombre sea-green gaze inscrutable.

GRAHAM R. TOMSON (1863-1911)
From 'To My Cat'

MANGO WITH MOLYNEUX
Joan Freestone
. . . .

CHAPTER THREE

Tiger! Tiger!

God made the cat that man might have the
pleasure of caressing the tiger. *Ferdinand Méry*

THE GINGER CAT
Gertrude Halsband
. . . .

*G*entlemen, I used to have a cat here, by the name of Tom Quartz, which you'd a took an interest in I reckon – most anybody would. I had him here eight year – and he was the remarkablest cat *I* ever see. He...had more hard, natchral sense than any man in this camp – 'n' a *power* of dignity – he wouldn't let the Gov'ner of Californy be familiar with him. He never ketched a rat in his life – 'peared to be above it.

MARK TWAIN (1835-1910)
From *Roughing It*

SAM, THE ALL AMERICAN CAT
Robert Macaulay

*A*nd now with a terrible deafening mew,

Like a Tiger I leap on my prey,

And just when I think I have torn it in two

It is in the air and away.

OLIVER HERFORD (1863–1935)
From 'The Game'

FIRST-CENTURY ROMAN MOSAIC
(detail)

There once were two cats of Kilkenny

Each thought there was one cat too many;

So they fought and they fit,

And they scratched and they bit,

Till, excepting their nails

And the tips of their tails,

Instead of two cats there weren't any.

ANONYMOUS

CATS FENCING
Louis Wain

For I will consider my Cat Jeoffrey.

For he is the servant of the Living God,

duly and daily serving him.

• • •

For having consider'd God and himself he

will consider his neighbour.

For if he meets another cat he will kiss her in kindness.

• • •

For he is of the tribe of Tiger.

For the Cherub Cat is a term of the Angel Tiger.

CHRISTOPHER SMART (1722-71)
From 'Jubilate Agno'

BEYOND THE ILEX
Derold Page
. . . .

*M*ice amused him, but he usually considered them too small game to be taken seriously; I have seen him play for an hour with a mouse and then let him go with a royal condescension.

CHARLES DUDLEY WARNER (1829-1900)
From *Calvin*

THE APPLE-MOUSE
Ditz

. . . .

Tiger! Tiger! burning bright
In the forests of the night,
What immortal hand or eye
Could frame thy fearful symmetry?

WILLIAM BLAKE (1757-1827)
From 'The Tiger'

PENNY BLACK AND TIFFANY TORTOISESHELL
Martin Leman

. . . .

*S*he moved through the garden in glory because

She had very long claws at the end of her paws.

Her neck was arched, her tail was high.

A green fire glared in her vivid eye;

And all the Toms, though never so bold,

Quailed at the martial Marigold.

RICHARD GARNETT (1835-1906)
'Marigold'

CAT WITH SPIDER
Jillian Peccinotti
. . . .

As in her ancient mistress' lap,

The youthful tabby lay,

They gave each other many a tap,

Alike dispos'd to play.

But strife ensues. Puss waxes warm,

And with protruded claws

Ploughs all the length of Lydia's arm,

Mere wantonness the cause.

WILLIAM COWPER (1731-1800)
From 'Familiarity Dangerous'

GIRL CHASTISING THIEVING CAT
Kuniyoshi

I am the cat of cats. I am
The everlasting cat!
Cunning, and old, and sleek as jam,
The everlasting cat!
I hunt the vermin in the night –
The everlasting cat!
For I see best without the light –
The everlasting cat!

WILLIAM BRIGHTY RANDS (1823–82)
'The Cat of Cats'

CAT WITH FISH
Indian painting (Kalighat)
. . . .

I have (and long shall have) a white great nimble cat,

A king upon a mouse, a strong foe to the rat,

Fine eares, long taile he hath, with Lions curbed clawe,

Which oft he lifteth up, and stayes his lifted pawe,

Deepe musing to himselfe, which after-mewing showes,

Till with lickt blood, his eye of fire espie his foes.

SIR PHILIP SIDNEY (1554-86)
From *Second Eclogues of Arcadia*

WHITE CATS WATCHING GOLDFISH
Arthur Heyer

Among human beings a cat
is merely a cat; among
cats a cat is a prowling
shadow in a jungle.

KAREL CAPEK (1890-1938)
From *I Had a Dog and a Cat*

CAT IN GRASS
Jane Ormes

*S*he sights a Bird – she chuckles –
She flattens – then she crawls –
She runs without the look of feet –
Her eyes increase to Balls –

Her Jaws stir – twitching – hungry –
Her Teeth can hardly stand –
She leaps, but Robin leaped the first –
Ah, Pussy, of the Sand,

The Hopes so juicy ripening –
You almost bathed your Tongue –
When Bliss disclosed a hundred Toes –
And fled with every one –

EMILY DICKINSON (1830-86)

CAT AND CANARY
Will Barnet

Cleanliness in the cat world is usually a virtue put above godliness.

CARL VAN VECHTEN
From *The Tiger in the House*

TWO CATS
Franz Marc
. . . .

The cat is domestic only as far as suits its own ends; it will not be kennelled or harnessed nor suffer any dictation as to its goings-out or comings-in.

"SAKI" (1870–1916)

TWO CATS
Nineteenth-century hooked rug

CHAPTER FOUR

A Clowder of Cats

If you want to be a psychological novelist and write about human beings, the best thing you can do is to keep a pair of cats. *Aldous Huxley*

CATCH THAT CAT
Monika Beisner

I love cats because I enjoy my home; and little by little, they become its visible soul.

JEAN COCTEAU (1889–1963)

WINSOR AND NEWTON
Martin Leman

Cats are a mysterious kind of folk.
There is more passing in their
minds than we are aware of.

SIR WALTER SCOTT (1771-1832) letter to
Washington Irving

A FEAST IN FAIRYLAND
Jigsaw by Louis Wain for Raphael Tuck & Son, 1909

*N*o matter how much cats fight, there always seem to be plenty of kittens.

ABRAHAM LINCOLN (1809-65)

THE ARTIST'S AWAY
R. W.

*L*overs most passionate, scholars austere
Both love, when their autumnal season falls,
Strong, gentle cats, majestic, beautiful;
They, too, sit still, and feel the cold night air.

• • •

They dream and take the noble attitudes
Of sphinxes lazing in deep solitudes,
Which seem to slumber in an endless dream. . . .

CHARLES BAUDELAIRE (1821-67)
From 'The Cats'

THREE FRIENDS ON KASAI MAT
Derold Page

Some pussies' coats are yellow;

some amber streaked with dark;

No member of the feline race

but has a special mark.

This one has feet with hoarfrost tipped;

that one has tail that curls;

Another's inky hide is striped;

another's decked with pearls.

ANONYMOUS

DOUBLE CAT-SPREAD
Ditz

Refined and delicate natures understand the cat. Women, poets and artists hold it in great esteem, for they recognize the exquisite delicacy of its nervous system; indeed, only coarse natures fail to discern the natural distinction of the animal.

CHAMPFLEURY (1821-89)

WOODEN CATS
Janet Thorndike

If you say 'Hallelujah' to a cat, it will excite no fixed set of fibres in connection with any other set and the cat will exhibit none of the phenomena of consciousness. But if you say 'Me-e-at', the cat will be there in a moment...

SAMUEL BUTLER (1835-1902)
From *Notebooks of Samuel Butler*

TWO CATS
Jillian Peccinotti
. . . .

*W*ild beasts he created later,
Lions with their paws so furious;
In the image of the lion
Made he kittens small and curious.

HEINRICH HEINE (1797-1856)
From 'Songs of Creation'

CATS
C. Raaphorst

*U*nknown to me, the whole feline population of London learnt that Miss Beauty of Catshire was to marry the illustrious Puff, who bore the Austrian colours...We found the cats of the district had come to congratulate me and to beg me to join their Ratophil Society. They explained to me that it was thoroughly common to chase rats and mice.

HONORÉ DE BALZAC (1799-1850)
From *The Love Affairs of an English Cat*

UNTITLED
Artist unknown

CHAPTER FIVE

Requiescat

O heaven will not ever Heaven be
Unless my cats are there to welcome me.

EPITAPH IN A PET CEMETERY

Cat! who hast pass'd thy grand climacteric,

How many mice and rats hast in thy days

Destroy'd? How many tit bits stolen? Gaze

With those bright languid segments green, and prick

Those velvet ears – but pr'ythee do not stick

Thy latent talons in me – and upraise

Thy gentle mew – and tell me all thy frays,

Of fish and mice, and rats and tender chick.

JOHN KEATS (1795-1821)
From 'On Mrs Reynolds' Cat'

THE CHAIRMAN
Louis Wain
. . . .

Pet was never mourned as you

Purrer of the spotless hue,

Plumy tail, and wistful gaze

While you humoured our queer ways,

Or outshrilled your morning call

Up the stairs and through the hall –

Foot suspended in its fall –

While expectant, you would stand

Arched to meet the stroking hand;

Till your way you chose to wend

Yonder, to your tragic end.

THOMAS HARDY (1840-1928)
From 'Last Words to a Dumb Friend'

BLACK CAT
Carole Thomson
. . . .

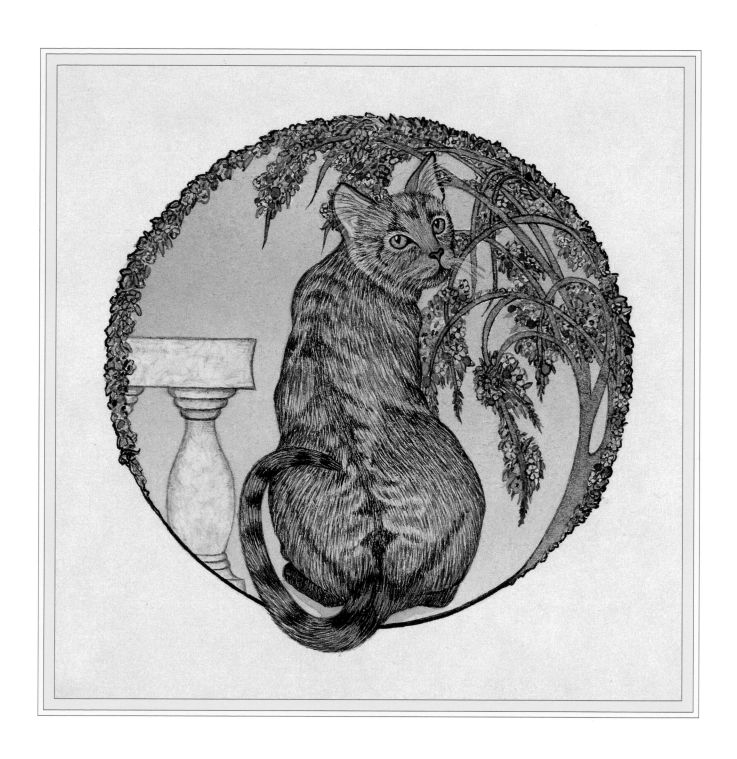

And art thou fallen, and lowly laid,
The housewife's boast, the cellar's aid,
Great mouser of thy day!
Whose rolling eyes and aspect dread
Whole whiskered legions oft have fled
In midnight battle fray.
There breathes no kitten of thy line
But would have given his life for thine.

ANONYMOUS
'Lament for Tabby'; or, 'Cat's Coronach'

THE CHURCH CAT'S DREAM
Derold Page

Puss passer-by, within this simple tomb

Lies one whose life fell Atropos hath shred;

The happiest cat on earth hath heard her doom,

And sleeps for ever in a marble bed.

Alas! what long delicious days I've seen!

FRANÇOIS DE LA MOTHE LE VAYER (1588–1672)
From 'Epitaph on the Duchess of Maine's Cat'

WICKER CHAIR
E. B. Watts

I never shall forget the
indulgence with which he
treated Hodge, his cat; for
whom he himself used to go out and buy
oysters, lest the servants having that trouble
should take a dislike to the poor creature. . .
I recollect him one day scrambling up
Dr Johnson's breast... and when I observed he
was a fine cat, saying, 'Why, yes, Sir, but I have
had cats whom I liked better than this'; and
then, as if perceiving Hodge to be out of
countenance, adding, 'but he is a very fine cat,
a very fine cat indeed.'

JAMES BOSWELL (1740-95)
From *Life of Dr Samuel Johnson*

THE NEW COLLAR
Nineteenth-century engraving

My golden love is kept for two,

That share my fire and mat;

A little dog with simple ways,

And my self-conscious cat.

W. H. DAVIES (1871-1940)
From 'Three Loves'

JACK RUSSELL AND PERSIAN
F. Rutherford
. . . .

Dear Furry Shade! In regions of the Dead,

On pleasant plains, by numerous waters, led;

What placid joys your brindled bosom swell!...

O dearly loved! untimely loss! – to-day

An offering at your phantom feet I lay:

Purr fond applause, and take in gracious kind

This little wreath of various verses twined;

Nor, though Persephone's own Puss you be,

Let Orcus breed oblivion – of me.

GRAHAM R. TOMSON (1863-1911)
From 'Dedication'

MINNIE FROM THE OUTSKIRTS
OF THE VILLAGE
R. P. Thrall

Come cats and kittens everywhere,

Whate'er of cat the world contains,

From Tabby on the kitchen stair

To Tiger burning in his lair

Unite your melancholy strains;

• • •

De Marsay dead! and never more

Shall I behold that silky form

Lie curled upon the conscious floor

With sinuous limbs and placid snore,

As one who sleeps through calm and storm.

• • •

And (when we've adequately moaned),

For all the world to wonder at,

Let this great sentence be intoned:

No cat so sweet a mistress owned;

No mistress owned so sweet a cat.

J. K. STEPHEN (1859-92)
'Elegy on de Marsay'

COVEN OF CATS
Janet Thorndike
. . . .

ACKNOWLEDGEMENTS

Quarto would like to thank the following for their help with this publication and for permissions to reproduce copyright material.

p.2 Esther Walton; p.6 Pippa Sterne; p.8 Bonhams; p.11 Bridgeman/Hanson Collection; p.13 Bonhams; p.15 Bridgeman/Private Collection; p.17 Bridgeman/Roy Miles Gallery; p.19 Bridgeman/Bonhams; p.21 E.T. Archive/Erika Bruce Collection; p.23 Bridgeman/Bonhams; p.25 Bridgeman/Josef Mensing Gallery; p.27 Emma Goss; p.29 Sally Holmes/Camden Graphics; p.30 E.T. Archive/Private Collection; p.33 Bridgeman; p.35 Bridgeman/Galerie George; p.37 E.T. Archive/Private Collection; p.39 Sally Hunter Fine Art; p.41 Bridgeman Art Library/Private Collection; p.43 Rosalind Stoddard; p.45 Bridgeman/Elgin Court; p.47 Martin Leman; p.49 Bridgeman/Private Collection; p.51 Edward Topsell/Bodleian Library; p.53 Christies; p.55 Will Barnet; p.57 E.T. Archive; p.60 Bridgeman/Private Collection; p.61 Bridgeman/Elgin Court; p.63 E.T. Archive/Private Collection; p.65 E.T. Archive; p.67 Bridgeman/Bonhams; p.69 Bridgeman/Private Collection; p.71 Bridgeman/Private Collection; p.73 Martin Leman; p.75 E.T. Archive; p.77 E.T. Archive; p.79 E.T. Archive; p.81 Bridgeman/Stern Art Dealers; p.83 Jane Ormes; p.85 Will Barnet; p.87 Bridgeman/Offentliche Kunstsammlung; p.89 American Museum, Bath; p.90 Monika Beisner; p.93 Martin Leman; p.95 E.T. Archive/Private Collection; p.97 Bridgeman/Eaton Gallery; p.99 Bridgeman/Private Collection; p.101 Bridgeman/Private Collection; p.103 Janet Thorndike; p.105 E.T. Archive; p.107 Bridgeman/Whitford and Hughes; p.109 Mary Evans; p.110 Bridgeman/Private Collection; p.113 E.T. Archive/Private Collection; p.115 E.T. Archive/Private Collection; p.117 Bridgeman/Rona Gallery; p.119 Bridgeman/Artist's Collection; p.121 Mary Evans; p.123 E.T. Archive/Michael Parkin Gallery; p.125 E.T. Archive/Shelbourne Museum Vermont; p.127 Janet Thorndike.

Every effort has been made to trace and acknowledge all copyright holders.
Quarto would like to apologize if any omissions have been made.